The Affairs of Dilys Willis

Dilys Willis	An almost ordinary housewife. She is completely and all-consumingly obsessed with cleaning. She will clean anything that will stand still long enough. Although her actions are incomprehensible to others, they are always perfectly logical to her. She cannot understand why others, including her husband, think she is crazy.
Mr Olmanroyd	A vacuum cleaner demonstrator and salesman. He is suffering from the malady of being in the wrong place at the wrong time.
Ronald Willis	Dilys' long-suffering husband. For once he has something to worry about, other than his wife's eccentricities.
Sheila	Ronald's sister. She is deeply upset. She is also deeply dizzy.
Charles	Sheila's husband. Because of Sheila's dizziness, he has had to spend the entire day in a pub. He is more than a little drunk.

ORIGINAL CAST

Dilys Willis .... Fran Walker
Mr Oldmanroyd .... Rob Darby
Ronald Willis .... Tom McHale
Sheila .... Anne McHale
Charles .... David Walker

Directed by David Walker

The Affairs of Dilys Willis

General Playing Notes

All the characters must be played straight for the comedy to work to it's full potential. Under no circumstances should the cast register any reaction to anything other than their own situation.

Scene: *The lounge of the Willis house. It is beautifully decorated and spotlessly clean. For a short time after the tabs open, the room is deserted. DILYS enters carrying a pair of men's trousers over her arm. She walks dreamily to the front and sighs.*

DILYS: That was fantastic. It was total ecstasy. The most wonderful ten minutes of my life. *(She turns and looks off left)* How was it for you Mr Oldmanroyd?

OLDMANROYD: *(Off)* Can I have my trousers back please, Mrs Willis?

DILYS: Not yet.

OLDMANROYD: *(Off)* But I have three other ladies to see this afternoon. Please give me my trousers back.

DILYS: All in good time Mr Oldmanroyd. All in good time.

(OLDMANROYD enters, wearing a bath towel around his lower regions)

OLDMANROYD: Look, Mrs Willis, I came here in good faith to demonstrate our latest vacuum cleaner model, which I have done. I did not expect to be thrown to the ground and have my trousers forcibly removed. I just came here to do my job.

DILYS: And very well you did it too, Mr Oldmanroyd. I have every intention of buying your magnificent machine.

OLDMANROYD: Why?

DILYS: Why what?

OLDMANROYD: Why do you want to buy the vacuum cleaner?

DILYS: Because it is a state of the art, top of the range, piece of equipment. The very best vacuum cleaner on the market.

OLDMANROYD: But Mrs Willis, you already have eleven vacuum cleaners.

DILYS: Twelve actually. There's one in the loft with a broken fan belt that my husband refuses to have mended.

OLDMANROYD: Then why, in the name of sanity, do you want another one?

The Affairs of Dilys Willis

(DILYS walks towards Oldmanroyd with purpose)

DILYS: Sit down, Mr Oldmanroyd.

OLDMANROYD: I don't want to sit down, Mrs Willis. I just want my trousers back on my legs, where they belong, so that I can get on with trying to earn my living.

(DILYS moves Oldmanroyd firmly to a chair and sits him down)

DILYS: I feel I owe you an explanation as to why I removed your trousers without your permission, Mr Oldmanroyd, and I think you'd take it better sitting down.

OLDMANROYD: I really don't have the time for this.

DILYS: Is that towel comfortable enough for you?

OLDMANROYD: Not it is not.

DILYS: Excellent. Then I'll begin. Mr Olmanroyd, I am a very fastidious person. I believe implicitly, that all things should be kept permanently clean. Dirt and grime are enemies of us all and I, for one, am not going to succumb to their evil influences. Not many people realise that, as soon as you stop cleaning something, it immediately starts to get dirty again. Now, with me this rarely happens. I have discovered that if I keep cleaning everything around me on a rotational basis, dirt and grime don't get the chance to attack. Am I making sense to you, Mr Oldmanroyd?

OLDMANROYD: Not in the slightest.

DILYS: Now Ronald, my husband, is not of the same opinion, I'm afraid. Ronald is a good man, Mr Oldmanroyd. A good man. If anyone should dispute this fact, I would... dispute it with them. He is kind, considerate, and above all, relatively docile. However, Ronald does have a problem.

OLDMANROYD: And I've got a pretty good idea what it is.

DILYS: Ronald has got it into his head that my desire to keep things clean is an obsession. He seems to think that it's not healthy for me to be constantly cleaning. In fact, and this will amaze you, he's so convinced that I have an obsession that he insisted that I went to see one of those Psychodelicist people.

OLDMANROYD: Psychiatrist?

The Affairs of Dilys Willis

DILYS: That's the chap. Do you know him?

OLDMANROYD: Not personally, no.

DILYS: A nice man. A very pleasant chap. But I feel that, as a doctor, he has serious limitations. *(Intimately)* Between you and me, Mr Oldmanroyd, he's as puddled as they come. *(She gives a knowing wink)* Anyway, he said that unless I make an effort to stop cleaning I will be in danger of going mad. Me, mad. I ask you, have you ever heard anything so ridiculous in all your life? I'm the sanest person I've ever met. Unfortunately, Ronald, my husband, agreed with this Psychodelicist chap and insisted that I get one of those domestic persons to do the cleaning for me. He hired this lady to come in two mornings a week. Can you imagine only cleaning the brass, glass and nick-knacks twice a week? Now that's madness for you.

OLDMANROYD: Mrs Willis, what has any of this got to do with you kidnapping my trousers?

DILYS: I'm coming to that. You see, I sent the cleaning lady packing after an argument over her attitude towards dusting the garden fence and now all is peace and harmony again with me in total control of the war against dirt and grime.

OLDMANROYD: Pardon me for being revisionary about this, but we seem to have drifted some way off the subject of my trousers, Mrs Willis.

DILYS: Not at all. I need your trousers, which incidentally need washing, I need your trousers as an insurance policy against a little favour I want you to do for me.

OLDMANROYD: Favour? What sort of favour?

DILYS: I want to purchase that wonderful vacuum cleaner of yours. The moment the transaction is completed, I shall return your trousers to you.

OLDMANROYD: Is that all?

DILYS: That is all.

OLDMANROYD: Well then, that's wonderful news. I'll give you the vacuum cleaner, you give me the money and my trousers and I'll bid you good afternoon.

DILYS: Would that it were that simple, Mr Oldmanroyd. You see, Ronald, my husband, won't allow me to have cash in case I should do something like...

let's say, buy another vacuum cleaner. Therefore, I shall have to pay for that wonderful machine by cheque, with a banker's card of course.

OLDMANROYD: Mrs Willis, right at this moment, with unwanted fresh air circulating around my nether regions, I would accept a cheque accompanied by a Mothercare season ticket! Now if you will kindly write the cheque and return my trousers, I will leave this house faster than a three-legged chicken.

DILYS: Once again a slight technical difficulty presents itself.

OLDMANROYD: Now what's wrong?

DILYS: The cheque book is in the inside pocket of my husband's jacket, which, in turn, is attached to him. And he's at work.

OLDMANROYD: Let me get this straight. You want to buy the vacuum cleaner to add to your collection.

DILYS: Correct.

OLDMANROYD: You have no cash at all in the house.

DILYS: Correct again.

OLDMANROYD: You can't pay by cheque because your husband...

DILYS: Ronald.

OLDMANROYD: Ronald, yes. Your husband has the cheque book and he's at work. If you ask him to write you a cheque for the cleaner, when he comes home, refusal is an absolute certainty in view of the fact that he thinks you are pathologically addicted to cleaning.

DILYS: You're catching on, Mr Oldmanroyd.

OLDMANROYD: The solution is simple, Mrs Willis. Don't buy the vacuum cleaner.

DILYS: There now, doesn't that just prove how wrong you can be? There was I thinking that you were catching on, and suddenly you slip away again. I can buy the vacuum cleaner, Mr Oldmanroyd, and I will buy the vacuum cleaner.

OLDMANROYD: With what? Monopoly money?

DILYS: We are now coming to the reason why I have temporarily relieved you of your trousers. Ronald will be arriving home from work soon. Very soon, in fact.

OLDMANROYD: Oh my God. For pity's sake, give me my trousers, Mrs. Willis. If your husband walks in here and sees me sitting, wrapped in his bath towel, minus my lower clothing, he could very well jump to the wrong conclusion.

DILYS: Exactly.

OLDMANROYD: What?

DILYS: At last you've got it.

OLDMANROYD: Got what? *(A thought dawns on him)* Oh no, Mrs Willis. Whatever is in that weird mind of yours, forget it.

DILYS: When Ronald comes in, the first thing he'll do is take his jacket off and hang it on the back of that chair. He's well trained you see. When he sees you sitting there, semi-clad, he's bound to ask for further information.

OLDMANROYD: Further information? I think he's more likely to run me through with a bread knife.

DILYS: Nonsense. Ronald's not like that. Besides, he knows better than to make that kind of mess on my carpet. When he asks who you are, I shall tell him that you are my secret lover.

OLDMANROYD: What? Are you mad?

DILYS: At that point you will stand up and exit hastily upstairs to the bedroom.

OLDMANROYD: The bedroom?

DILYS: Correct. Ronald is sure to follow you. If he doesn't, I shall tell him that you have mistreated me and that he should go and have a word with you upstairs, where it's quiet.

OLDMANROYD: This is completely insane.

DILYS: No, it isn't, it's brilliant. Because while he's upstairs, discussing the situation with you, I shall take the cheque book from the inside pocket of his jacket and write out the cheque for the vacuum cleaner. Now what could be simpler than that?

OLDMANROYD: Mrs Willis, I don't know whether this is some kind of practical joke, but if it is, it's in very poor taste. And if it isn't, then it's the most outrageous suggestion I've ever heard. Now, I have had quite enough of this nonsense and I insist that you hand over my trousers this instant.

The Affairs of Dilys Willis

(DILYS looks out of the window)

DILYS: Too late.

OLDMANROYD: What do you mean, too late?

DILYS: The dye is cast, Mr Oldmanroyd. Ronald is walking up the garden path right at this minute.

OLDMANROYD: Oh my God.

(DILYS drapes the trousers over the back of a chair)

DILYS: That's where he puts his jacket. He can't fail to notice your trousers. The plot is on.

OLDMANROYD: This is all a hideous nightmare. I'll wake up in a minute. Please God let me wake up in a minute.

RONALD: *(Off)* Dilys, I'm home.

OLDMANROYD: Now would be a good time to wake me up, God.

(RONALD enters and goes to DILYS and kisses her on the cheek)

DILYS: Hello dear. Have a nice day at the office?

RONALD: Absolutely dreadful. You would not believe what happened today.

DILYS: Why don't you take your jacket off and hang it on your usual chair, on top of that man's trousers?

RONALD: Thank you.

(RONALD takes his jacket off and drapes it over the trousers)

I've heard something today that will absolutely devastate you.

DILYS: Really, dear. Why don't you sit on the sofa, next to that man who's not wearing any trousers, and tell me all about it.

(RONALD sits and looks at Oldmanroyd)

RONALD: Good evening.

(OLDMANROYD is stuck in a frozen stare. RONALD sits next to him)

It's Charles.

DILYS: No, it isn't. It's Mr Oldmanroyd. He's my secret lover and he's not wearing any trousers.

RONALD: He's walked out on Sheila. They had a silly little row and he packed

The Affairs of Dilys Willis

a suitcase and left. My poor little sister.

DILYS: Oh dear. That's a knotty little problem, isn't it?

RONALD: It's not a problem, Dilys, it's a catastrophe. *(He turns to Oldmanroyd)* Sheila's my baby sister.

(OLDMANROYD nods dumbly)

She's not very strong at the best of times. This has devastated her.

DILYS: Don't worry, Ronald, once she's had a good session with her vacuum cleaner, she'll be as right as domestos.

RONALD: Oh, Dilys. The vacuum cleaner is not a panacea for all ills. *(He pauses abruptly and stares at Dilys)* Have you been cleaning today?

DILYS: Not at all dear. I've been too busy with Mr Oldmanroyd here.

RONALD: Because you know what the doctor said.

DILYS: Mr Oldmanroyd visits me twice a week, while you're out at work. That's why he's not wearing any trousers.

(RONALD stands and walks up to Dilys and stands face to face with her)

RONALD: Dilys, I want you to swear to me that you have not been cleaning. You'll never get better if you weaken.

DILYS: Would you smile at me Ronald?

RONALD: What?

DILYS: I just want to see your wonderful smile.

(Confused, RONALD smiles meekly)

Wider, please.

(RONALD smiles wider. As he does, DILYS takes a toothbrush out of her apron pocket and polishes his teeth. RONALD reacts)

RONALD: No, Dilys, no. You must not do that.

DILYS: They needed cleaning. You haven't done them since this morning.

RONALD: *(Putting his hands on her shoulders)* Dilys, listen to me. You are my wife.

DILYS: Yes, I know.

RONALD: When I said the words of our wedding vows all those years ago,

The Affairs of Dilys Willis

specifically the bit about better and worse, I actually meant them.

DILYS: I've never doubted that for one minute, Ronald.

RONALD: You have a problem, a serious mental problem, and as your loving husband it is my duty to see that you do everything possible to overcome your little obsession. *(Turns to Oldmanroyd)* Quite a large obsession, actually.

OLDMANROYD: Yes, I'd noticed.

RONALD: So please, Dilys, please. Stop cleaning.

DILYS: I'll try, dear. I'll do anything to please you; except give up my passionate affair with Mr Oldmanroyd here.

(DILYS drags the reluctant Mr Oldmanroyd to his feet. For the next few speeches she constantly moves him into Ronald's eye line)

RONALD: Excellent. Now, what was I talking about? Oh yes, Sheila. I hope you don't mind, Dilys, but I've invited her round for dinner this evening. She was in such a frightful state on the telephone, I felt I had to do something.

DILYS: Very commendable of you, Ronald. We'll have a cosy little foursome. You, Sheila, me and Mr Oldmanroyd. Unfortunately, Mr Oldmanroyd hasn't got any trousers on. I do hope that won't make Sheila go all nostalgic, now that Charles has gone.

RONALD: I can't understand why he should have just up and left like that. According to Sheila, there hasn't been any arguments. Well, no more than is usual for those two. I know Charles is a bit rough and ready, compared to the rest of the family, but I really never thought he'd do anything like this. I wonder what brought it on?

DILYS: Perhaps once a month wasn't enough for him.

RONALD: Once a month? What are you talking about?

DILYS: Well, rumour has it that she only does a daily spring clean once a month.

RONALD: Dilys, this has nothing to do with cleaning.

DILYS: I wouldn't be so sure. Last time I was round there I distinctly saw a thin layer of dust on the front door step. And as for the guttering...

RONALD: Dilys, stop that. Sheila's cleaning routine has nothing to do with Charles walking out on her.

The Affairs of Dilys Willis

DILYS: Suit yourself. We know better, don't we Mr Oldmanroyd?

(OLDMANROYD breaks free from Dilys and flops down on the sofa with head in his hands)

OLDMANROYD: This is not happening to me. Somebody please tell me this is not happening to me.

(The door bell rings)

RONALD: That'll be Sheila now. Please Dilys, promise me you won't mention the front door step or the guttering.

DILYS: If you insist. Although someone's got to tell her sooner or later.

(RONALD exits to open the front door)

DILYS: Now's my chance.

(She heads for the jacket and starts to rummage through the inside pocket)

OLDMANROYD: Mrs Willis, this situation has gone from the sublime to the surreal. I don't care whether I'm wearing trousers or not; I'm getting the hell out of here.

DILYS: Don't be ridiculous, Mr Oldmanroyd. You can't walk the streets without your trousers. This is a respectable neighbourhood.

(RONALD re-enters, accompanied by SHEILA, who is obviously distressed. DILYS tries to get her hand out of the inside jacket pocket but, in fact, she has put her hand in OLDMANROYD'S trouser pocket by mistake. She quickly sits with her hand firmly jammed)

DILYS: Oh hello Ronald, you're back. Sheila, how lovely to see you. Have you dusted your front step yet?

(SHEILA bursts into tears)

RONALD: Dilys, I asked you not to mention that.

DILYS: Ooops, sorry.

(With a supreme effort DILYS wrenches her hand free from OLDMANROYD'S trousers. As she does there is a horrible ripping sound, as the two legs of the trousers part company with each other)

OLDMANROYD: Ahh!!! My trousers.

DILYS: Oh dear, look at that Ronald. I've accidentally ripped Mr Oldmanroyd's

The Affairs of Dilys Willis

trousers. That's what you get for being over passionate with me, Mr Oldmanroyd.

RONALD: Dilys, can't you see that Sheila's very distressed? Come and sit on the sofa, Sheila. *(He leads SHEILA to the sofa. When he gets there he addresses Oldmanroyd)* Would you mind awfully moving up a bit, please?

DILYS: This is Mr Oldmanroyd, Sheila. He's my secret lover. He's not wearing any trousers just at the moment.

(OLDMANROYD sits, head in hands, embarrassed)

RONALD: You mustn't get yourself too upset, Sheila. Any man who does what Charles has done to you doesn't deserve tears.

SHEILA: I just don't understand it. Why would he want to walk out on me? I've been a good wife to him Ronald. I've cooked him meals, ironed his clothes and brought up his children. I even clean the house once a month.

DILYS: What did I tell you?

RONALD: Dilys, please.

DILYS: I rest my case.

SHEILA: I ask you, as a man, Ronald, what more could a man want?

RONALD: There's nothing else a man could want, Sheila. I only wish Dilys cleaned our house once a month, instead of once every ten minutes.

SHEILA: The events of this morning will be engraved on my memory for the rest of my life.

RONALD: Exactly what happened?

SHEILA: Well, we'd had a little disagreement about the table cloth.

DILYS: There's nothing more off-putting than a dirty table cloth.

SHEILA: It wasn't dirty. At least, it wasn't dirty before Charles came down to breakfast. You see, he went out with his friends last night, to the pub. I don't mind him going to the pub, so long as he stays sober, but last night he had far too much to drink. I can always tell when he's had too much to drink, he always... does something in the bidet. Anyway, he came down to breakfast very quietly and poured out his cornflakes. *(She starts to cry again)* I was only trying an experiment.

RONALD: What sort of experiment?

The Affairs of Dilys Willis

SHEILA: The salt cellar broke last night and so I put the sugar in the jar marked coffee, because we don't drink coffee, and put the salt in the jar marked sugar. Charles likes a lot of sugar on his cornflakes.

RONALD: Oh dear.

SHEILA: He vomited all over my clean table cloth. When I asked him why he had done it, he simply said something very rude and ran upstairs. When he came down, half an hour later, he had a suitcase with him. He shouted at me, Ronald. He told me I was a half-witted, feather-brained moron. Then he shouted, "Goodbye, I'm off" and he and the suitcase slammed the door and were gone. *(She cries again)* And I'm all alone and heart-broken.

RONALD: That's dreadful. Isn't that dreadful, Dilys?

DILYS: I'll say. Even cornflakes with salt on is no excuse for vomiting over a clean table cloth.

RONALD: What are we going to do about him?

SHEILA: I've already done something about him.

RONALD: What?

SHEILA: I went to see Phillip next door. He's a locksmith. Twenty minutes after he left, every lock in the house had been changed. Then I went to Mother's to cry.

RONALD: You did the right thing, Sheila.

SHEILA: Mother didn't think so. She told me to pull myself together and go home.

RONALD: I mean changing the locks. You want to make sure that unmitigated scoundrel can't get back into your house. If I ever see him again, I'll give him a jolly good beating.

DILYS: Then let's hope you don't see him, dear. Let's face it, you would have difficulty giving a runny egg a jolly good beating.

RONALD: Believe me, Dilys, when my gander is up, I'm a positive savage.

DILYS: Really? I'd never noticed.

RONALD: Sheila, dear, why don't you stay with Dilys and me for a few days, until you get over the shock of all this?

DILYS: Good idea. While you're here I could give you some tips on how to keep your front step clean.

RONALD: Dilys, you're not helping Sheila.

DILYS: I could though. I could teach her how to be a little more hygienic about the house. That way maybe she'll keep her men.

(SHEILA cries louder. RONALD goes to her)

RONALD: Don't listen to her, Sheila. She's only joking.

DILYS: I'm not.

RONALD: You come into the kitchen with me and we'll have a nice cup of tea.

DILYS: Ah, the British answer to every problem. Let's have a nice cup of tea. Excuse me, Madam, but I'm afraid your house has just exploded. Never mind, let's have a nice cup of tea.

(RONALD moves behind Dilys)

RONALD: I wish you'd show a little more concern about Sheila's problem.

DILYS: I'm concerned, I'm concerned.

(RONALD picks his jacket from the chair and puts it on. DILYS looks annoyed)

Why are you putting your jacket on? You're only going to the kitchen.

RONALD: Dilys, this is serious business. I cannot possibly feel serious without my jacket.

(RONALD helps Sheila to her feet and leads her into the kitchen)

DILYS: Drat. There goes another chance to get my hands on that cheque book.

(OLDMANROYD rises and moves to Dilys)

OLDMANROYD: Mrs Willis, you have torn my trousers completely in half.

DILYS: We must think of some way to get that cheque book.

OLDMANROYD: This stupid idea of yours is a complete failure. I've been sat on that sofa without any trousers on since your husband walked in, and he hasn't even noticed. What planet is he from?

DILYS: Sometimes he takes a little time to catch on.

OLDMANROYD: Catch on?

DILYS: Perhaps it would help if you took something else off.

The Affairs of Dilys Willis

OLDMANROYD: No!!

DILYS: Take your shirt off, Mr Oldmanroyd. He's bound to notice you then.

OLDMANROYD: Under no circumstances, Mrs Willis, and I'd be very grateful if you would give some serious consideration to how you're going to repair my trousers.

DILYS: Staples.

OLDMANROYD: Staples? Are you crazy?

DILYS: Ronald always carries a stapler in his briefcase.

(DILYS goes to the briefcase)

OLDMANROYD: You can't mend trousers with staples.

DILYS: It'll be fine, so long as you don't sit down.

OLDMANROYD: Mrs Willis, you can't drive a car standing up.

DILYS: Oh no. He's put the combination lock on his briefcase, and I don't know the combination.

OLDMANROYD: Thank heaven for small mercies.

DILYS: I know. Cellotape. There's some in my dressing table drawer. Shan't be long, Mr Oldmanroyd.

(DILYS exits to the bedroom)

OLDMANROYD: For God's sake, Mrs Willis, don't leave me on my own with no trousers on. Oh no. This is ridiculous.

(The door bell rings. OLDMANROYD looks stunned)

RONALD: *(Off)* Answer the door please, Dilys.

DILYS: *(Off)* Answer the door please, Mr Oldmanroyd.

OLDMANROYD: Oh my God!

(The door bell rings more insistently)

RONALD: *(Off)* Hurry up and answer the door, Dilys.

DILYS: *(Off)* Hurry up and answer the door, Mr Oldmanroyd.

(OLDMANROYD groans, tightens the towel around his waist, and exits to the front door)

CHARLES: *(Off)* Where is the silly cow?

The Affairs of Dilys Willis

RONALD: *(Off)* Who is it, Dilys?

DILYS: *(Off)* Who is it, Mr Oldmanroyd?

OLDMANROYD: *(Off)* Er... who are you, please?

CHARLES: *(Off)* I am Charles.

OLDMANROYD: *(Off)* It's Charles, Mrs Willis.

DILYS: *(Off)* It's Charles, Ronald.

RONALD: *(Off)* Charles? Oh no.

(CHARLES enters. He is obviously a little drunk. OLDMANROYD enters after him, trying not to be seen)

CHARLES: Sheila, where are you, you dozy Herbert?

(DILYS enters from the bedroom, carrying a roll of cellotape)

DILYS: Hello, Charles. How are you?

CHARLES: Where's that cloth-brained bint I'm unfortunate enough to be married to?

OLDMANROYD: I don't think there's any need for comments like that.

CHARLES: Don't you indeed? Well perhaps you haven't spent all day in a...., who the bloody hell are you?

DILYS: This is Mr Oldmanroyd, Charles. He's my secret lover.

CHARLES: *(Looking at Oldmanroyd closely)* He hasn't got any trousers on.

OLDMANROYD: At last, somebody's noticed.

(Enter RONALD and SHEILA)

RONALD: What are you doing here, Charles?

(CHARLES turns and falls over the chair. He staggers to his feet)

CHARLES: I'll tell you what I'm doing here. I'm looking for her.

(CHARLES moves towards Sheila. As he does, he falls over the chair again. He stares at the chair)

Will you sod off out of the way.

RONALD: Charles, are you drunk?

CHARLES: Of course I'm drunk. You don't think I'd keep falling over the same

The Affairs of Dilys Willis

chair if I was sober, do you?

SHEILA: Charles, we have nothing to say to each other.

CHARLES: Haven't we, indeed? Well, I've got plenty to say to you, you stupid woman. For instance, why won't my key fit the front door?

SHEILA: Because I've had all the locks changed.

CHARLES: What the hell for?

RONALD: Now calm down, Charles, we don't want a scene.

CHARLES: A scene?

SHEILA: Yes. A scene like the one you made this morning, just because you put a little bit of salt on your cornflakes.

CHARLES: A little bit? There was enough salt on my cornflakes to defrost North Wales.

SHEILA: That's still no excuse for walking out on me.

CHARLES: Walking out on you? What are you talking about?

SHEILA: You left with a suitcase and slammed the door. That's what I call walking out on me. That's why I've had the locks changed.

CHARLES: I only went to buy a paper.

DILYS: Oh dear.

SHEILA: Then why did you pack your suitcase?

CHARLES: I didn't. The suitcase was empty. I've lent it to Frank at the newsagents to go on holiday with.

SHEILA: But I thought...

CHARLES: You thought? I've had to spend the whole day in the pub because you thought. You stupid cow.

RONALD: I will not stand by and hear my sister abused like this.

CHARLES: Well sit down then.

RONALD: I told you at the time, Sheila, you should never have married this lout. You are nothing but a cad, sir. A cad, I say.

DILYS: Is this the positive savage you were telling me about, Ronald?

RONALD: I've got a good mind to give you a damn good thrashing, you villain.

The Affairs of Dilys Willis

SHEILA: Don't you dare lay one finger on my husband.

CHARLES: That's it, Sheila. You tell him.

RONALD: But Sheila, I'm only trying to protect you. The man is a screwball.

SHEILA: How dare you talk about screwballs. Especially when you're married to the biggest screwball of them all.

RONALD: What did you say, Sheila?

CHARLES: Yeh. When it comes to screwballs, your Dilys is the top of the premier league, mate.

RONALD: How dare you. Dilys is completely cured. She hasn't bought a vacuum cleaner for three weeks, have you dear?

DILYS: Not yet.

SHEILA: I know you're my brother Ronald, but when it comes to insulting my husband, I won't let anyone get away with it.

(SHEILA moves and puts her arm around Charles)

RONALD: I can't believe I'm hearing this.

CHARLES: You'd better believe it, mate. We're a team. And a bloody good one too. Why don't you take your wacky missus and crawl back into your hole, you snivelling little creep?

SHEILA: You tell him, Charles.

RONALD: Right that does it. My gander is up. Put your fists up, sir, and we'll settle this like men.

CHARLES: Find me a man to fight and I'll put up my fists.

(CHARLES and SHEILA laugh. RONALD puts up his fists. CHARLES, in a cavalier fashion, pushes Sheila to one side and does the same. They circle around each other like bad boxers. OLDMANROYD, who has been standing against the back wall, moves forward between them)

OLDMANROYD: Now gentlemen, this is all a simple misunderstanding, I'm sure there's no need for a punch up.

(CHARLES lunges wildly at RONALD. He misses him by a mile, but catches OLDMANROYD full on the chin. OLDMANROYD falls over the sofa and on to the forestage. RONALD drops his guard and walks up to Charles. He

The Affairs of Dilys Willis

laughs in his face)

RONALD: Missed me. You couldn't hit an elephant with a railway sleeper, you drunken slob.

(CHARLES picks up one of a matching pair of vases and hits RONALD over the head with it. RONALD giggles briefly before falling over the sofa on to the opposite side of the forestage to Oldmanroyd)

DILYS: Oh, good shot, Charles.

(CHARLES moves to Sheila and puts his arm around her)

CHARLES: That's shut him up for a while. Shall we go home, dear?

SHEILA: Yes, darling.

(They turn to exit through the front door)

CHARLES: Have you got your key with you?

SHEILA: Yes, darling.

CHARLES: Good. Only mine won't fit in the lock you see.

(CHARLES and SHEILA exit. After a short pause, DILYS picks up the remaining vase)

DILYS: Now where am I going to find a match for this?

(Still holding the vase, she approaches RONALD and begins foraging in his inside pocket for the cheque book. As she does, RONALD starts to come to with a moan)

RONALD: Oh, Dilys.

(DILYS hits him over the head with the vase)

DILYS: That solves the problem of finding a match.

(She takes the cheque book and places it carefully on the table. She goes into her bag and gets out her cheque card and pen. She places them on the table with the cheque book and moves to OLDMANROYD. She gently slaps his face. He comes to with a groan)

Mr. Oldmanroyd, Mr. Oldmanroyd. Ah, good, you're back with us. Tell me, who do I make the cheque payable to?

(OLDMANROYD falls back with a groan)

BLACKOUT - TABS - THE END

EFFECTS

The lighting is constant early summer evening. There are no other effects.

PROPS

A pair of men's trousers for Dilys.

Cleaning utensils, (anything that Dilys can carry about her person)

A large pocketed apron for Dilys.

Canvassing folder for Mr Oldmanroyd.

Briefcase for Ronald.

Large, spotted handkerchief for Sheila.

Two matching, breakable vases. (made from papier mache)

Cheque book (in Ronald's jacket pocket)

Large roll of cellotape for Dilys

SET

Three doors required: Stage right door leads to the front door. Centre door leads upstairs. Stage Left door leads to the kitchen.

On the "fourth wall" there is a window which looks out onto the driveway.

Stage Right there is a sofa; stage Left there is an easy chair. Centre Right is a bureau and chair and on the back wall, to the Left of the Centre door, is a Welsh dresser.

The room is gaudily decorated, in keeping with Dilys' personality, and is spotlessly clean. Nothing is out of place.